THE Crayola SHAPES BOOK

MARI SCHUH

LERNER PUBLICATIONS ◆ MINNEAPOLIS

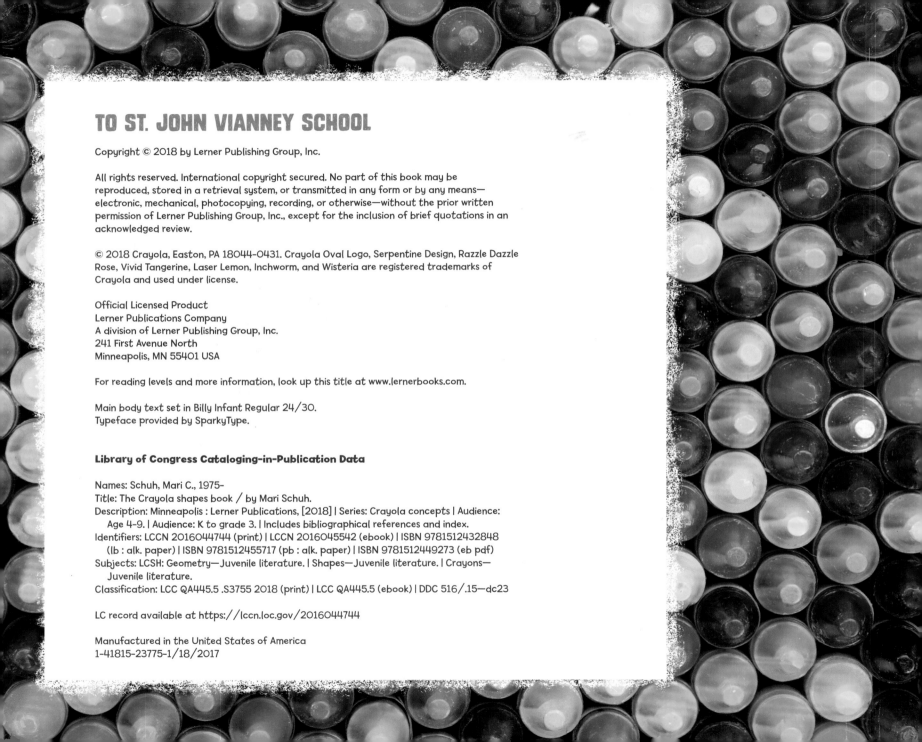

TO ST. JOHN VIANNEY SCHOOL

Official Licensed Product
Lerner Publications Company
A division of Lerner Publishing Group, Inc.
241 First Avenue North
Minneapolis, MN 55401 USA

For reading levels and more information, look up this title at www.lernerbooks.com.

Main body text set in Billy Infant Regular 24/30.
Typeface provided by SparkyType.

Library of Congress Cataloging-in-Publication Data

Names: Schuh, Mari C., 1975-
Title: The Crayola shapes book / by Mari Schuh.
Description: Minneapolis : Lerner Publications, [2018] | Series: Crayola concepts | Audience: Age 4–9. | Audience: K to grade 3. | Includes bibliographical references and index.
Identifiers: LCCN 2016044744 (print) | LCCN 2016045542 (ebook) | ISBN 9781512432848 (lb : alk. paper) | ISBN 9781512455717 (pb : alk. paper) | ISBN 9781512449273 (eb pdf)
Subjects: LCSH: Geometry—Juvenile literature. | Shapes—Juvenile literature. | Crayons—Juvenile literature.
Classification: LCC QA445.5 .S3755 2018 (print) | LCC QA445.5 (ebook) | DDC 516/.15—dc23

LC record available at https://lccn.loc.gov/2016044744

Manufactured in the United States of America
1-41815-23775-1/18/2017

Table of Contents

SHAPES ALL AROUND

Look high. Look low. Wherever you go, shapes are all around.

A shape is the form of an object. There are lots of different shapes!

LINES MAKE SHAPES

Shapes are made from lines.

This bike is made of circles and straight lines.

What can you draw with circles and straight lines?

Colorful flags hang in a market.
They are triangles.

How many sides does a triangle have?

You can hop on shapes! Play hopscotch alone or with your friends.

Squares are made of straight lines. Together, many squares make up a game of hopscotch. What can you draw with squares and straight lines?

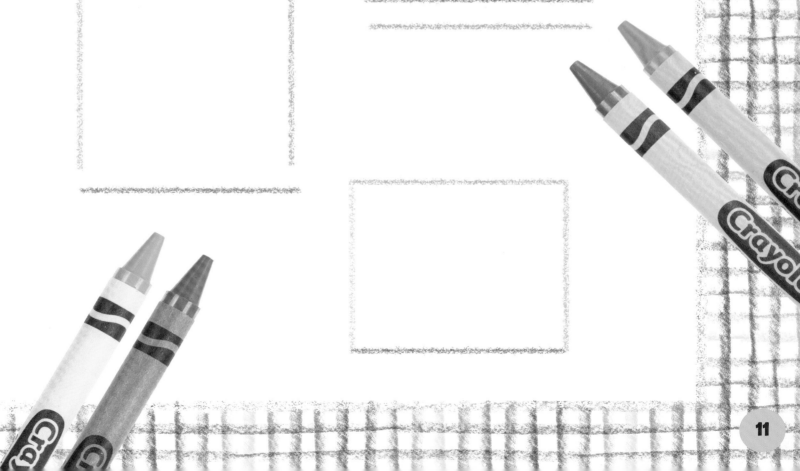

Rectangles are also made of straight lines.

A rectangle has two short sides and two long sides.

Animals have shapes too!

You can find sea stars on hot, sandy beaches.

Draw a big star with your favorite crayon. Then fill in the star by coloring with the side of the crayon. What does the star's texture look like?

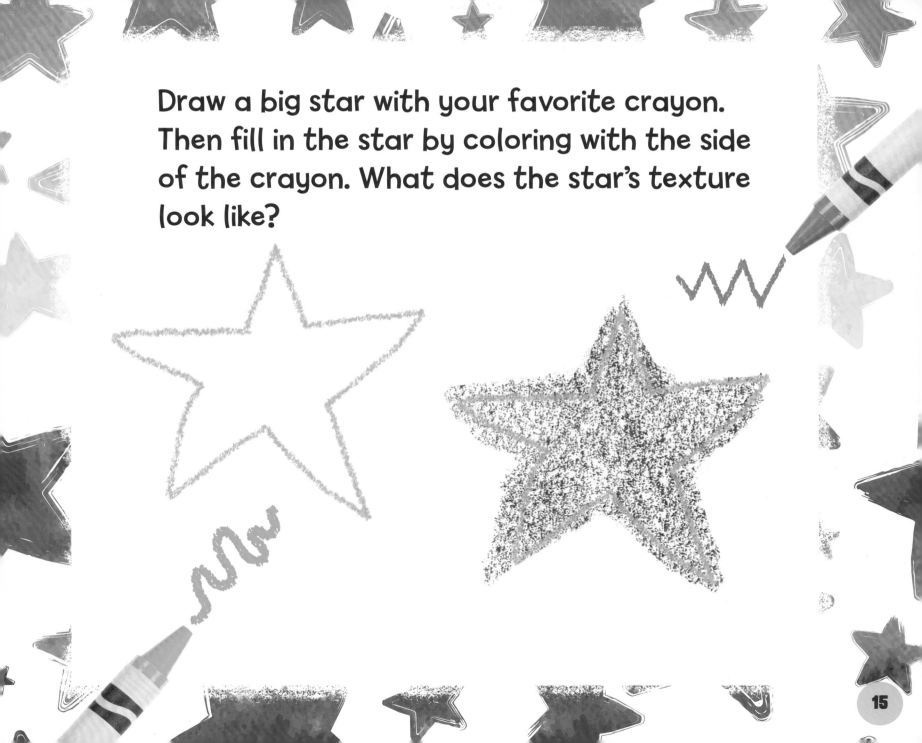

SOLID SHAPES

Solid shapes take up space.

Some solid shapes are round. Others have many sides.

What solid shapes can you find?

A cube is a solid shape with six faces.

Some of the robots' bodies are cubes. What solid shapes can you draw?

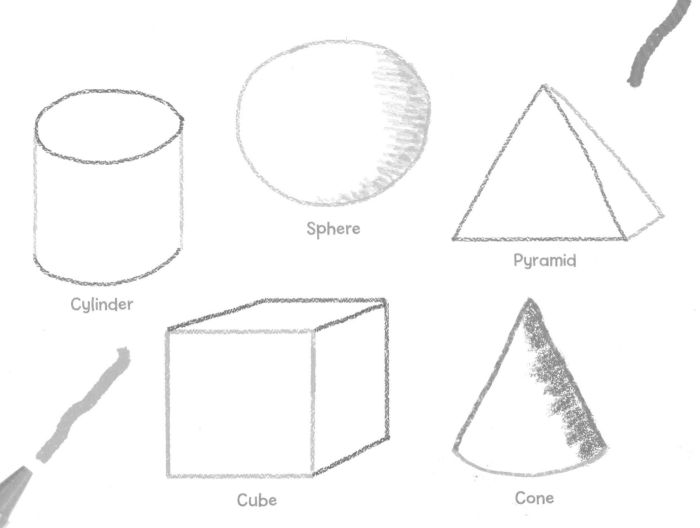

Cylinder

Sphere

Pyramid

Cube

Cone

FUN WITH SHAPES

There are many different shapes in the world. What shapes will you see today?

WORLD OF COLORS

Shapes come in all kinds of colors! Here are some of the Crayola® crayon colors in this book. Can you find them in the photos?

RAZZLE DAZZLE ROSE

VIVID TANGERINE

LASER LEMON

INCHWORM

SKY BLUE

PERIWINKLE

CORNFLOWER

WISTERIA

GLOSSARY

circle: a shape that is perfectly round

cube: a solid shape with six faces

flat: having a smooth or even surface

rectangle: a shape that has two short sides and two long sides

solid: having length, width, and thickness

square: a shape that has four equal sides

texture: the look and feel of an object

triangle: a shape with three sides

TO LEARN MORE

BOOKS

Brocket, Jane. *Circles, Stars, and Squares: Looking for Shapes*. Minneapolis: Millbrook Press, 2013. Find all sorts of shapes in this book—from circles and ovals to diamonds, cubes, and rings.

MacDonald, Suse. *Shape by Shape*. New York: Little Simon, 2009. Turn the pages of this book to learn more about shapes and see how they come together to form a creature from long ago.

Welzen, Jon. *I Know Shapes*. New York: Gareth Stevens, 2017. Read this book to learn about shapes, numbers, sizes, and sorting.

INDEX

WEBSITES

Hide 'n' Seek Geometric Shapes
http://www.crayola.com/crafts/hide-n-seek-geometric-shapes-craft/
Hide shapes inside a drawing, and then see if your friends and family members can find and name all the shapes that are hidden.

Magical Shape Hunt
http://pbskids.org/peg/games/magical-shape-hunt
Visit this website to play a shape-hunting game.

PHOTO ACKNOWLEDGEMENTS

The images in this book are used with the permission of: © Laurelie/Dreamstime.com, p. 5 (top left); © iStockphoto.com/mkos83, p. 5 (top right); © Gillian Hardy/Dreamstime.com, p. 5 (lower left); © iStockphoto.com/mactrunk, p. 5 (lower right); © iStockphoto.com/druvo, p. 5 (center); © iStockphoto.com/olaser, p. 6; © iStockphoto.com/chomphunuts, p. 9; © iStockphoto.com/123ducu, p. 13; © iStockphoto.com/Maica, p. 14; © Tanjulchik/Shutterstock.com, p. 15 (border of stars); © iStockphoto.com/tr3gi, p. 16; © iStockphoto.com/rrhatbruce, p. 17; © iStockphoto.com/ManuKro, p. 18; © alterfalter/Shutterstock.com, p. 20; © iStockphoto.com/sandoclr, p. 21 (top left); © iStockphoto.com/asikkk, p. 21 (top right); © iStockphoto.com/junpinzon, p. 21 (lower left); © Todd Strand/Independent Picture Service, p. 21 (lower right); © Nutpat Chaisinthop/Shutterstock.com, p. 21 (center).

Cover: © Vitaliy Stepanenko/Dreamstime.com (ferris wheel); © iStockphoto.com/SolStock (hopscotch squares); © alterfalter/Shutterstock.com (bubble gum machines); © Todd Strand/Independent Picture Service (color pencils).

LERNER
SOURCE

Expand learning beyond the printed book. Download free, complementary educational resources for this book from our website, www.lernerresource.com.